rocking

in the cradle

of the moment


fred andrle

# rocking
# in the cradle
# of the moment

haiku, senryu,
and small poems

# fred andrle

2019

For Marlene

Copyright © 2019 Fred Andrle
All rights reserved

ISBN 978-1-880977-48-4

Published 2019 by XOXOX Press,
Gambier OH 43022 USA

Haiga illustrations — Marlene Hyman
Book design — Jerry Kelly

Available at IngramSpark, your local independent bookshop, and on the web.
Booksellers, kindly order via Ingram.

Library of Congress Cataloging-in-Publication Data

Names: Andrle, Fred, author.
Title: Rocking in the cradle of the moment : haiku, senryu, & small poems /
  by Fred Andrle.
Description: Gambier, OH : XOXOXpress, 2018.
Identifiers: LCCN 2018046046 | ISBN 9781880977484
Subjects: LCSH: Haiku, American.
Classification: LCC PS3601.N5529 A6 2018 | DDC 811/.6--dc23
LC record available at https://lccn.loc.gov/2018046046

huge bumblebee
chasing you
you think



springtime carousel
the melody
of horses

all-night rain
circling moon
cradled sleep

the mule

more sure-footed

than my affections

strolling ease
of spring's first day
hand in caring hand


we sleep
the garden grows
all night

early spring
she's waiting for
the bloom and scent of roses



she calls the raccoons
kangaroos
kindergarten innocence

ego's urgencies
the blip of life

thunder

slams against my window

spring obstreperous

charged with light

the space

between our thoughts

felled

a hundred oaks

industrial forest

if you turn away
when I speak my truth
I'll become, once again,
the flowers


angry neighbor
calls police
childhood's end

leave me alone
I'll leave you alone
spring hornets' nest

desert night
falling star
fades into silence

hummingbird
moth
double
take


emerald spider
on your pant leg
look before you leap!

spattered

windshield

every

insect

life…

treetop cardinals
call and response
crimson liturgy


God's spare time
amusement:
warthog

he vanished
from his thoughts
clear lake contentment


little mouse
her run of the house
*may all beings be happy*

trimmers

in the alleyway

the scream of trees

your hand in mine

this single moment

only

wind turbine morning:
picking up
the kill


showering pink
the crabapple
surrenders her blossoms

to and fro
of tidal
sandpipers



clutching many grievances
he cannot
break his fall

transcontinental

monarch

garden-training

gazing far up
into mulberry branches
elder-adventure


crisp half-spring
the last snowflake
vanishes

chill rain morning
children laughing
anyway

he slowed to greet
the tortoise
of his life



spider lowering
off my hat brim
peaceful coexistence

little boy
your light-saber
a fallen maple twig

mouth:breast, crotch:tongue
he's looking for love
in all the wrong places

thundercloud
the beauty
of advancing darkness



toppled
garbage cans
of hound dog spring

arcing flight
of springtime geese
their glad cacophony



peering
down the well
engaging darkness

who am I?

he asked himself

the morning of his death

ecstatic sway

of maple branches

pay attention

watching an earnest bee
work my blossoming garden
I'm right here, right now



I've got to tell you
when you stomped on that spider
the afternoon dimmed

sawing down
the fractured oak
spring funereal



anger's ebb
the calm
of spirit's sea

tumult

of the public day

quietude of mind

student orchestra
fingering
every which way


phone calls
she makes
announcing death

astounding leaps
branch to branch
squirrel Olympiad!

ambition's drill
his military life

I'll stick with you
till I'm no longer
gooey


summer
at the railroad tracks
a golden salamander

swift the dawn,
the day, the dark
careening elderhood



gardening
she falls away
from herself

summer evening's
dark conundrum:
katy-did/katy-didn't

no worm
no hook
fishing innocent



the calming sea
the dragging net
the captured, dying beings

shoelace

comes undone

his calm acceptance

little girls

afternoon seesaw

giggling up and down

summer moves slowly
summer passes quickly
what do you think?



white butterfly
where do you shelter
from the dark rain?

balmy summer
wind set free
ballerina maples


that fly who roams
your evening kitchen:
leave a dirty dish in the sink

she lets fall

her garment of opinion

disrobing for peace

these gifts
the falling sun
the shadowed breezes



recalling
all life's gladness
happy deathbed

touching earth

earth

touching me

drift of clouds
beyond
the summer oak


Saturday confessional
bless you, father
have you sinned?

the hollering

the jabbering

crow-tree

hopes and dreams

of slaughterhouse cattle

strolling the country road
looking right, looking left
I never arrive



sudden fall
of summer rain
that wild calming

first firefly
flaring on the upswing
true summer


the backyard oak
drops a limb
like me, imperfect

the fiction

of your death

who could believe it?

fork-tail squirrel

so many

life stories

dog poop
on my summer sandal —
the unity of being!



evening light
a tradesman
trudges homeward

surrounded by vegetables
the farm market boy
picking his nose



summer flesh
the blare
of shirtlessness

rain-swept earthworm

blocks her path

she steps aside

afternoon departing
twilight
seeping into skin


little snake
the roadway claimed
golden flies attending

wisdom

of cavorting dogs

thought-less-ness

dreaming winter
in sullen summer


feel-good feet
massage the earth
meditation ramble

steady snail, persevering bee



little mouse
she buries
in the garden

pitching easy
soaring high
carefree softball summer


starry canopy
the river rat spots its gleam
in her new pups' eyes

guilt and fear

twin swords

of melancholy

the graveyard's calm

my mind's distress

can I find a happy medium?

children's voices
piercing sweet
her summer office window




strawberry moon
hiding
behind mulberry branches

the clarity
of blue summer
awakenings


sheltering maple
cardinal
hawk

the old man walks

sun or rain

for a little while longer

lilt

of summer air

the shadowed garden


too hot, too cold

too damp, too dry

the seasons humanized

crescent moon
the flare
of burning Venus

life's every moment
filtered through
belief

you, butterfly
called mourning cloak,
thanks for the reminder



the alligator
does not ponder
vegetarianism

drowsy lecture
summer
tapping at the window


chapel bell
establishing
the night

in my dreams
I beat you bloody
fifth grade bully Louie

he chanced upon
the summer
of his innocence



little spider
down the drain
forgive me, didn't notice

3am

I rise to

old-man-trickle

you say yes

I say no

immensity


*Party Pooper*

Chapter One

The Book of Introversion

shuttered bookstore
empty sidewalks
steel town afternoon

the roofer's shout
his busy hammer
August slowly failing


backyard birdbath
robin rinsing
the cleanliness of being!

one gaze

one touch

one thought

serenity

little fly

too swift to trap

mi casa tu casa

tell me you know me
like the bee knows the blossom
I'll be happy


my flung-forward mind
the present's steady energy

fledgling fallen
nest so high
little beating heart


circling forward, back
thumb-twiddling
time

dragon-fire:

the power

of her patience

she poops and eats
and smiles a lot
autumn elder-dog


silence
of the hayfield night
full moon

backyard Buddha
little garden peace

little tree
they chopped you down
beauty as nuisance




his father's
old binoculars
the autumn stars

kingfisher

helicoptering

over the fishy stream

TV weatherman
thrilling
at tornados


tug-o-war
dog and me
the treasured tennis ball

dragons of my youth

now silent metaphors

the carousel
the golden ring
his fallen horse



autumn dark
a candle
in the woods

every

instant

offering

grace

voice of thunder

distant

kingdoms

sunrise calm
that gladness
before thought




plucking petals
afterlife?
He loves me, loves me not

brain's discordant melodies
the doleful music
of dementia



autumn afternoon
he rides
the silences

everywhere I go

mother sun

brethren fields

howling in the alley
night cats
making love or war


he slap-kills
the brief mosquito
Great Mosquito flinches

grammar of

my expectations:

present tense

elder dog
at autumn ease
twilight porch commander


living
in his body
thought peripheral

those two white butterflies
are they dancing
or fighting?

cathedral spire
the sentience
of stone


greeting cats
of urban alleys
*trot, meow*

enchanted road trip

who knows

where it leads

his every thought

a sailing

from safe harbor

alligator swamp
the fate
of dragons


dark museum
little night mouse
contemplates Picasso

I will bury you, sweetheart,
or you will bury me
autumn turns winter



speak
love
now

love eternal

deep beyond thought

winter turns spring

worry

upon worry

he stacks them up

hounds of winter
lonely
at windows


this very instant
touched
by these, my fingers

winter thaw
triple squirrels
daredeviling on branches


*sit! speak!*
*down! roll over!*
brainwashing the dog

smiley billboard woman

mimicking

the deep heart

a hint of light
in winter's
dark compassion


exercise!
the tedium
of movement

our only recourse

*now*

lived buoyantly

wedding bed
she belches, farts
he comes to know
the secret life
of woman

winter thaw
neighbor kids
mud-puddling


evening light
that tilts the body
wistful

*bloody hell*
the sideways charm
of beguiling curses



relaxing
in the bliss
of self-acceptance

mourning dove

calling out

our sorrow

sullen gloom
or hush contemplative
choosing your winter




hound dog? friend
chicken? product
farmer schizophrenic

her coughing, sneezing

he loves her

but it's 4am

wind and hail
the old German Shepherd
turns away from the door




trumpeting over the plain
calling out a farewell
the last elephant

aiming for enlightenment
he thoroughly chews
the Snickers bar

slipping off

life's tattered garment

the serene elegance of dying

make the bed
take the step
praise the day


praying to no one
in particular
foxhole atheist

winter dawn
quarreling crows
irritate the silence




grieving fish
of jailhouse
aquariums

syllables retreating
just beyond his grasp
failed haiku

his elder-life:
the dragon
is reading


snore

sweat

stink

intimacy

mind
eclipsing
heart

serenity

of winter darkness

chapel of the stars

the many dachshunds
of the earth
global yap chorale



concealed within each musing
her long-dead father
poised to strike

arctic wolf, garden mole
the many shapes and lives
of spirit


in barren winter
give yourself
the great gift of love

he won't commit

he won't depart

her relationship sphinx

the slow river

forks around the tiny island

forever

shocking power:
thought's destructive
whirlwind


January thaw
bipolar winter

winter horse
pale stars
silent pasture




sidewalk penny
season-stained
the shrug of affluence

I like

I do not like:

four season misery

this world
of yes and no
her glad repose


quietly at the window
doing nothing
nothing doing

bile yellow

on winter white

canine watercolorist

dying
for our pleasure
all the earth




watching
a meandering snowflake's
tumble

beauty fades

a chance to glimpse

heart's loveliness

zebra

lion

paradise

lost


listening to his ego
    prattle
morning meditation

twilight rooftops
snowfall sparrows
winter in their wings

*now* infused

with *then* and *later*

Zen's imperfect tea

skipping on ice
OK with falls
winter-girls


nodding good morning
to the peaceable dead
cemetery stroll

winter thaw
the fragility
of hope




double rainbow
wakes your gladness
the heavens miss you so

trudging left to right

pedestrian

prose

slowing my step

to match

earth's leisurely rotation

comprehending death
he chooses
presence



rocking
in the cradle
of the moment

Fred Andrle is the author of two previous poetry collections, *Love Life* (XOXOX Press, 2008) and *What Counts* (XOXOX Press, 2012). For more than 20 years, Fred was executive producer and host of the public affairs radio talk show "Open Line," heard on WOSU, Columbus. You can read more of Fred's poetry at his website: fredandrle.com

Some of the haiku/senryu in this collection appeared previously in *Akitsu Quarterly, bottle rockets, Chrysanthemum, Failed Haiku, Frogpond, Haiku Foundation Per Diem, hedgerow, Presence,* and *World Haiku Review.*

Thanks to my fellow House of Toast Poets MJ Abell, Charlene Fix, Linda Fuller-Smith, Jerry Roscoe and Jacquelin Smith for their helpful suggestions and encouragement.

www.ingramcontent.com/pod-product-compliance
Lightning Source LLC
Chambersburg PA
CBHW071459080526
44587CB00014B/2152